SCOOBY-DOO!

A SCIENCE OF SOUND MYSTERY

by Megan Cooley Peterson   illustrated by Christian Cornia

A SONG FOR ZOMBIES

CAPSTONE PRESS
a capstone imprint

Scooby-Doo and the gang drove home after a long day at school.

"Man, I love my new music class," said Shaggy. "I could play this tambourine all day, every day."

Velma covered her ears. "I don't think my eardrums could take that."

"Watch out for those kids, Fred!" shouted Daphne.

Fred slammed on the brakes. "They don't look like kids at all," he said.

"What's going on here?" Velma asked an officer.

"All the kids in the neighborhood have been zombified," said the officer. "The adults are terrified."

"Rombified?" asked Scooby.

"Zombified? Like, what's zombifying them?" asked Shaggy.

The officer showed the gang a photograph. "This creature was spotted in the neighborhood late last night. Whenever it played the pan flute, children turned into zombies and followed it."

"I'm confused," said Shaggy. "The kids were asleep in their beds. How did the music get inside their houses?"

"Sound travels through air, water, and even walls, if it's loud enough," Daphne said.

"Sound is a kind of energy, like heat and light," Velma explained. "When something vibrates, like your vocal cords or an instrument, it makes sound waves. The waves cause molecules to move. As the molecules bump into each other, they make sound."

small wavelengths for high-frequency sound

large wavelengths for low-frequency sound

FACT FILE

Sound travels through the air at 1,129 feet (344 meters) per second. It travels through steel at 16,404 feet (5,000 m) per second.

"Sound waves move faster through denser materials like water and metal," Fred said. "The molecules are packed together closely. The sound waves pass more easily from molecule to molecule."

"You've lost me again," Shaggy said.

"Imagine this fence is a block long," Velma said. "If you held your ear to the fence at one end of the block, and I hit the fence with a hammer at the other end of the block, which ear do you think would hear the sound first?"

Shaggy scratched his head. "Like, the ear on the fence?"

"Right! The sound waves move much faster through metal than through air," Velma explained.

FACT FILE

In outer space there is no sound. There is no air or other material for sound waves to travel through.

"Man, I hope those creepy kids don't take over the neighborhood," Shaggy said.

"Re reither," agreed Scooby.

"Like, I need a snack and someplace to practice my tambourine," added Shaggy.

"Oh, brother," Velma muttered.

A girl tapped Fred's shoulder. "Hi, Fred. I wanted to remind you that we're meeting in the library after school."

"Thanks for tutoring me on my government homework, Sarah," Fred said. "See you then!"

"Zoinks!" shouted Shaggy when a passing teacher dropped a book with a bang. "That scared me!"

"You can uncover your pinna now," Velma said.

BLAM

"Did you say 'dinna'? I could go for some dinner!" Shaggy said, rubbing his stomach.

"No, *pinna*. It's your outer ear," Velma explained. "Its main job is to gather sound waves."

"Then the sound waves hit your eardrum," Fred continued. "The eardrum is a thin piece of tightly stretched skin. It turns sound waves into vibrations."

"Small bones move these vibrations to your cochlea," added Velma. "It's a small tube that sends sound signals to your brain."

Daphne crouched over the book. "Look! It's a drawing of that pan flute-playing zombie. I wonder why our new music teacher has it?"

"Only one way to find out," said Fred.

"Mr. Green?" asked Daphne. "Do you recognize this creature?"

"Ah, yes," he said. "According to the legend, this zombie plays the pan flute at night. Young children who hear its spooky song turn into zombies."

Scooby picked a pan flute off a table. "Ran rute!" he said and began to play.

"The pan flute is a rather unusual instrument. Is there a reason you have one?" Velma asked.

Mr. Green snatched the flute away from Scooby. "It's a souvenir from my travels. Now, please, go to your next class."

"Shaggy, why are you wearing earmuffs?" Daphne asked.

"Music has, like, magical powers!" exclaimed Shaggy. "I'm not taking any chances."

"Music doesn't have magical powers," Velma assured him. "But the earmuffs are still a good idea." She tugged on her earlobe and winced at Scooby's drumming.

"Stronger vibrations, like Scooby's drumming, make louder sounds," Daphne explained. "And weaker vibrations make softer sounds."

"As sound passes through a material, some of it gets absorbed," said Fred. "The molecules in your earmuffs catch some of the sound waves."

"Your earmuffs will easily absorb softer sounds, like a whisper," said Velma.
"But they won't absorb loud sounds as much."

Scooby kept banging on the drums. "No kidding!" shouted Shaggy.

"And soft surfaces absorb sounds better than hard surfaces," Velma added.
"That's why walking on carpet sounds quieter than walking on a hardwood floor."

"Let's search for clues tonight at Mr. Green's house," said Fred.
"I think that music man is hiding something."

FACT FILE

Place your hand on your throat
and whisper. Then speak loudly.
Can you feel your throat vibrating
at different strengths?

"Like, do we really have to be here?" asked Shaggy. "It's so dark and creepy."

"Mr. Green and the police officer both said the zombie plays only at night," Velma said. "If Mr. Green is responsible, we can catch him in the act."

Shaggy pointed toward a shadowy figure. "Not if that zombie gets us first!"

"What are you kids doing sneaking around out there? Come inside," Mr. Green said.

"We thought you might be the zombie," Daphne admitted.

Mr. Green shook his head. "I assure you, I am no zombie."

Suddenly, music drifted into the house. "Did you hear that?" asked Shaggy. "The zombie's playing the pan flute!"

"Let's go, gang!" shouted Fred. "I have a plan to catch that zombie."

"This is humiliating," said Shaggy. "Why are we dressed up like little kids?"

"The zombie targets children," explained Fred. "We'll simply lure the zombie using you and Scooby as bait."

"Ruh, roh," said Scooby.

"We'll hide up on the porch," Daphne said. "When you see the zombie, speak into this cup."

"Like, how does that work?" asked Shaggy.

"The sound waves will travel through the string to the other cup," Velma said. "We'll be able to hear what you say."

"Then we'll trap that zombie!" exclaimed Fred.

"Man, that thunder is spookier than any zombie," said Shaggy. "Why is it so loud?"

"Thunder is a huge sound wave," said Daphne. "When lightning strikes, it heats up the air around it."

"The heated air expands quickly," continued Velma. "The expanding air creates sound waves. And that makes thunder."

"Luckily, the storm is passing. Quick, everyone into position!" said Fred.

Just then the zombie started
playing its terrible tune. Soon
the zombie children surrounded
Scooby and the gang.

"The zombie has invited its
friends!" shouted Daphne.

"Zoinks!" cried Shaggy.
"Let's get out of here!"

"Like, all this zombie business is making me hungry," Shaggy said.

"Re roo," agreed Scooby.

"I can hardly even hear the zombie's creepy music anymore," said Shaggy. "What a relief!"

"That's because sound waves lose energy as they travel," Velma explained.

"Velma's right," said Daphne. "The farther away you get from a sound's source, the quieter it gets. Eventually you can't hear it at all."

FACT FILE

Have you ever heard a loud boom as an airplane passes overhead? A shock wave forms behind a plane that is flying faster than the speed of sound. When this wave passes you, it sounds like a boom.

"So, like, what about sirens on an ambulance?" asked Shaggy. "Right after it passes by, the siren sounds lower, not quieter."

"That's called the Doppler effect," Fred said. "As the ambulance moves, the sound waves in front get bunched together. The sound waves behind get stretched out."

"Once it passes you, the siren sounds lower," added Velma. "That's because the stretched-out sound waves have a lower frequency."

"Yeah, that *is* freaky!" said Shaggy.

"Not *freaky*. Frequency," Fred corrected. "And a lower frequency means a lower pitch."

"Well, science sure sounds *freaky* to me," said Shaggy.

"Hee, hee, hee, hee!" Scooby laughed.

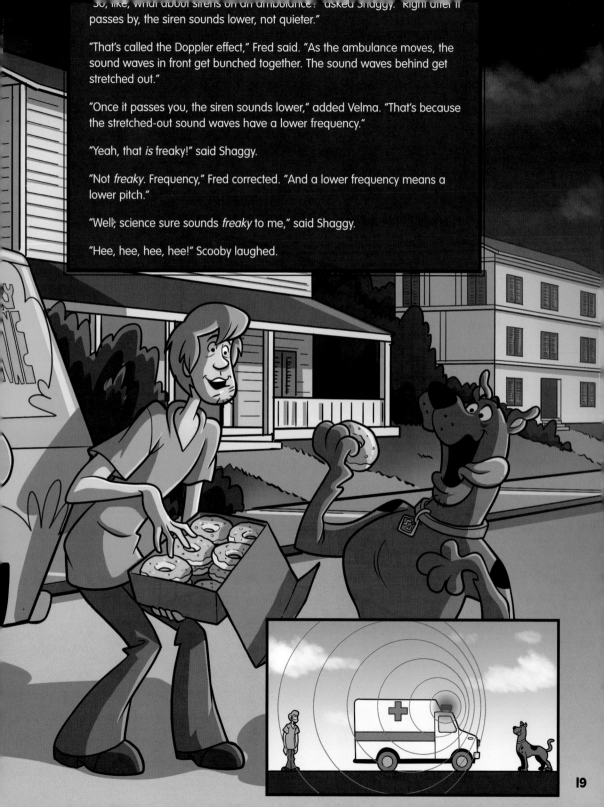

19

"Something about those zombie children doesn't sit right with me," Fred said.

Velma plugged her music player into the Mystery Machine's speakers. "We need a closer look at those kids. I downloaded some pan flute music. Maybe it will lure the zombie children to us."

"Rombies?" Scooby said, spraying donut crumbs.

"Turn up the volume," added Daphne. "Let's make it as loud as possible."

"Is there, like, a tiny musician playing inside that speaker?" Shaggy joked.

"Electricity from my player passes into magnets inside the speaker," Velma explained. "The magnets vibrate a cone made of paper. The cone makes these vibrations louder before sending the sound waves toward your ears."

"It's working!" cried Fred. "Here come those creepy kids!"

"Can I have a donut?" asked one of the children as he took off a mask.

"Like, what is going on here?" Shaggy asked.

"We thought you kids had been turned into zombies!" cried Daphne.

The kid bit into the donut. "We were only pretending," he said. "My neighbor paid us in candy to act like zombies."

"I knew there was something off-key about this," said Velma.

"I found Scooby's old dog whistle the other day," said Velma. "If the zombie is actually a human in disguise, it won't be able to hear the whistle."

"Like, why not?" asked Shaggy.

"Dogs can hear higher frequencies than people can," explained Daphne. "Maybe the same is true for zombies?"

"Look! There's the zombie!" yelled Fred.

"Let's check this zombie's hearing," Velma said, blowing the whistle.

"Rouch!" shouted Scooby.

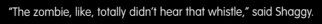

"The zombie, like, totally didn't hear that whistle," said Shaggy.

"Which means it's definitely human," added Fred.

"Scooby, can you catch that fake zombie?" Daphne asked.

"Res!" said Scooby, galloping toward the zombie.

FACT FILE

Sounds are measured in units called hertz. One hertz equals one vibration per second. The human ear can hear frequencies from about 20 hertz to 20,000 hertz. Dogs can hear from about 60 hertz to 60,000 hertz. A dog whistle is usually about 22,000 hertz.

"Time to see who this zombie really is," said Daphne. Scooby pulled off the zombie's mask.

"Sarah?" asked Fred. "Is that you?"

"Yes," the girl admitted. "I was trying to scare away all the adults so I could run this town."

"But why?" Velma asked.

"I'm really good at government class, remember?" Sarah asked Fred. "I have brilliant ideas on how to govern this city, but adults won't let kids be in charge! I learned about the pan flute zombie in Mr. Green's music class."

"Things are beginning to make sense," said Daphne.

"And I would've gotten away with it if it weren't for you meddling kids!" Sarah shouted.

"But *you're* a kid," Shaggy said.

"Don't remind me," Sarah muttered.

"Well, gang," Fred said. "Now that we've solved the pan flute mystery,
how about we grab some *pan*cakes?"

"That's, like, music to my ears," Shaggy said, licking his lips.

GLOSSARY

cochlea (KOH-klee-uh)—a spiral-shaped part of the ear that helps send sound messages to the brain

Doppler effect (DAH-pluhr uh-FEKT)—the way wave frequency seems to change depending on how a source of waves, such as a siren, and an observer move toward or away from each other

electricity (i-lek-TRIS-i-tee)— the movement of electrons that can be used to make light and heat or to make machines work

energy (EN-uhr-jee)—the ability to do work, such as moving things or giving heat or light

frequency (FREE-kwuhn-see)—the number of sound waves that passes a location in a certain amount of time

molecule (MOL-uh-kyool)—the atoms making up the smallest unit of a substance; H_2O is a molecule of water

pinna (PIN-uh)—the outer part of the ear

pitch (PICH)—the highness or lowness of a sound; low pitches have low frequencies and high pitches have high frequencies

shock wave (SHOK WAYV)—a burst of quickly moving air

vibration (vye-BRAY-shuhn)—a fast movement back and forth

SCIENCE AND ENGINEERING PRACTICES

1. Asking questions (for science) and defining problems (for engineering)

2. Developing and using models

3. Planning and carrying out investigations

4. Analyzing and interpreting data

5. Using mathematics and computational thinking

6. Constructing explanations (for science) and designing solutions (for engineering)

7. Engaging in argument from evidence

8. Obtaining, evaluating, and communicating information

Next Generation Science Standards

READ MORE

Milios, Rita. *Sound in the Real World.* Science in the Real World. Minneapolis: ABDO Publishing, 2013.

Thomas, Isabel. *Experiments with Sound.* Read and Experiment. Chicago: Heinemann Raintree, 2015.

Wacholtz, Anthony. *Mummies and Sound.* Monster Science. North Mankato, Minn.: Capstone Press, 2014.

INTERNET SITES

FactHound offers a safe, fun way to find Internet sites related to this book. All of the sites on FactHound have been researched by our staff.

Here's all you do:

Visit *www.facthound.com*

Type in this code: 9781515725930

Super-cool stuff!

Check out projects, games and lots more at
www.capstonekids.com

INDEX

Thanks to our adviser for his expertise, research, and advice:
Paul Ohmann, PhD, Associate Professor of Physics
University of St. Thomas, St. Paul, Minnesota

Published in 2016 by Capstone Press, A Capstone Imprint
1710 Roe Crest Drive, North Mankato, Minnesota 56003
www.mycapstone.com

Library of Congress Cataloging-in-Publication Data
Names: Peterson, Megan Cooley, author.
Title: Scooby-Doo! a science of sound mystery : a song for zombies / by Megan Cooley Peterson.
Description: Science of sound mystery | North Mankato, Minnesota : Capstone
Press, a Capstone imprint, [2016] | 2016 | Series: Scooby-Doo!.
Scooby-Doo solves it with S.T.E.M. | Includes bibliographical references
and index. | Audience: ages 9-12. | Audience: grades 4 to 6.
Identifiers: LCCN 2015043266 | ISBN 9781515725930 (library binding) | ISBN 9781515726548 (ebook PDF)
Subjects: LCSH: Sound—Juvenile literature. | Scooby-Doo (Fictitious
character)—Juvenile literature.
Classification: LCC QC225.5 .P45 2017 | DDC 534—dc23
LC record available at http://lccn.loc.gov/2015043266

Editorial Credits
Editor: Kristen Mohn
Designer: Ashlee Suker
Creative Director: Nathan Gassman
Production Specialist: Gene Bentdahl
The illustrations in this book were created digitally.

Printed in the United States of America.
032016   009681F16

OTHER TITLES IN THIS SET:

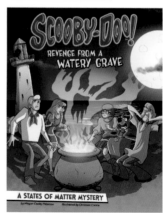